TRADITIONAL SONGS

The Farmer in the Dell

Edited by Ann Owen

Illustrated by Sandra D'Antonio

Music Consultant:
Peter Mercer-Taylor, Ph.D.
Associate Professor of Musicology,
University of Minnesota,
Minneapolis, Minnesota

Reading Consultant: Susan Kesselring,
M.A., Literacy Educator
Rosemount-Apple Valley-Eagan
(Minnesota) School District

PICTURE WINDOW BOOKS
MINNEAPOLIS, MINNESOTA

Traditional Songs series editor: Peggy Henrikson
Page production: The Design Lab
Musical arrangement: Elizabeth Temple
The illustrations in this book were rendered in pen with digital coloring.

PICTURE WINDOW BOOKS
5115 Excelsior Boulevard
Suite 232
Minneapolis, MN 55416
1-877-845-8392
www.picturewindowbooks.com

Printed in the United States of America.
1 2 3 4 5 6 08 07 06 05 04 03

Library of Congress Cataloging-in-Publication Data
The farmer in the dell / edited by Ann Owen ; illustrated by Sandra D'Antonio.
p. cm. — (Traditional songs)
Summary: Provides a history and words to ten verses of the folk song, "The Farmer in the
Dell," as well as simple instructions for making a musical instrument and playing the
traditional game. Includes bibliographical references (p.).
ISBN 1-4048-0149-9 (library binding)
1. Children's songs, English—United States—History and criticism—Juvenile literature.
2. Folk songs, English—United States—History and criticism—Juvenile literature. [1. Folk
songs—United States. 2. Singing games. 3. Games.] I. Owen, Ann, 1953- II. D'Antonio,
Sandra, 1956- ill. III. Series.
ML3551.F25 2003
782.42162'13'00268—dc21
2002155299

What do you see when you sing a song? Does the music come in colors?

What do you do when you sing a song? Does the melody make you dance?

What do you hear when you sing a song? Do the words tell a story?

Let's explore the sights and sounds of one of our favorite songs.

Who's with the farmer down in the dell?

Children form a circle with one child as "the farmer" in the middle. They join hands and sing, while circling around the farmer. The farmer chooses someone to join him or her in the center as "the wife." Then "the wife" chooses someone to be "the child." As the song continues, the group in the center joins hands and circles in the direction opposite the outer circle's dancing. On the last verse, the child chosen to be "the cheese" stands alone, as the rest of the children in the center join the outer circle. He or she then becomes the farmer for the next round.

The farmer
in the dell,
the farmer
in the dell,
heigh-ho,
the derry-o,
the farmer
in the dell.

The farmer takes a wife, the farmer takes a wife,
heigh-ho, the derry-o, the farmer takes a wife.

The wife takes a child, the wife takes a child,
heigh-ho, the derry-o,
the wife takes a child.

The child takes a nurse, the child takes a nurse, heigh-ho, the derry-o, the child takes a nurse.

The nurse takes a dog, the nurse takes a dog,
heigh-ho, the derry-o, the nurse takes a dog.

The dog takes a cat, the dog takes a cat,
heigh-ho, the derry-o, the dog takes a cat.

The cat takes a rat, the cat takes a rat,
heigh-ho, the derry-o, the cat takes a rat.

The rat takes the cheese, the rat takes the cheese,
heigh-ho, the derry-o, the rat takes the cheese.

The cheese stands alone, the cheese stands alone,

heigh-ho, the derry-o, the cheese stands alone.

The farmer in the dell, the farmer in the dell,
heigh-ho, the derry-o, the farmer in the dell.

The Farmer in the Dell

The far - mer in the dell,___ the far - mer in the dell,

Heigh - ho, the der - ry - o, the far - mer in the dell.___

2. The farmer takes a wife, the farmer takes a wife,
   Heigh-ho, the derry-o, the farmer takes a wife.

3. The wife takes a child, the wife takes a child,
   Heigh-ho, the derry-o, the wife takes a child.

4. The child takes a nurse, the child takes a nurse,
   Heigh-ho, the derry-o, the child takes a nurse.

5. The nurse takes a dog, the nurse takes a dog,
   Heigh-ho, the derry-o, the nurse takes a dog.

6. The dog takes a cat, the dog takes a cat,
   Heigh-ho, the derry-o, the dog takes a cat.

7. The cat takes a rat, the cat takes a rat,
   Heigh-ho, the derry-o, the cat takes a rat.

8. The rat takes the cheese, the rat takes the cheese,
   Heigh-ho, the derry-o, the rat takes the cheese.

9. The cheese stands alone, the cheese stands alone,
   Heigh-ho, the derry-o, the cheese stands alone.

10. The farmer in the dell, the farmer in the dell,
    Heigh-ho, the derry-o, the farmer in the dell.

About the Song

Many songs that Americans love began in Europe. People who came to America in the late 1800s brought "The Farmer in the Dell." At that time, it was called "The Farmer's in His Den." *Den and dell* both mean a clearing in the woods.

"The Farmer in the Dell" and other songs like it are singing games. They are sometimes called ring dances. The players make their own music by singing and clapping. Singing games have been played for hundreds of years in countries all over the world.

DID YOU KNOW?

Artists have been painting dancers for more than 600 years. In 1340, an Italian artist named Ambrogio Lorenzetti did one of the earliest known paintings of a group of dancers. The painting shows nine people holding hands and dancing in a ring. A tenth person is playing the tambourine. This scene is part of a larger wall painting called "The Effects of *Good Government*."

Make a Hands-Free Musical Instrument for Dancing

WHAT YOU NEED:

• 1 piece of narrow elastic about 7 inches (18 centimeters) long
• a marker in your favorite color (if you have white elastic)
• 5 medium-size jingle bells

WHAT TO DO:

1. Color one side of the elastic with the marker, unless your elastic is a color already.
2. String the jingle bells onto the piece of elastic through the top loop on each bell.
3. Tie the ends of the elastic so the loop is big enough when stretched to go over your hand. You want it to fit your wrist snugly but not too tightly. You may wish to wear your bells on your ankle. If so, adjust the size to fit.
4. Wear your bells when you dance to "The Farmer in the Dell" or any other singing game or dance.

To Learn More

AT THE LIBRARY

Krull, Kathleen. *Gonna Sing My Head Off!: American Folksongs for Children*. New York: A.A. Knopf, 1992.

Murphy, Andy. *Out and About at the Dairy Farm*. Minneapolis: Picture Window Books, 2003.

O'Brien, John, Illustrator. *The Farmer in the Dell*. Honesdale, Pa.: Boyds Mills, 2000.

Schuh, Mari C. *Dogs on the Farm*. Mankato, Minn.: Capstone Press, 2002.

Wallner, Alexandra, Illustrator. *The Farmer in the Dell*. New York: Holiday House, 1998.

ON THE WEB

CHILDREN'S MUSIC WEB
http://www.childrensmusic.org
For resources and links on children's music for kids, parents, educators, and musicians

NATIONAL INSTITUTE OF ENVIRONMENTAL HEALTH SCIENCES KIDS' PAGES: CHILDREN'S SING-ALONG SONGS
http://www.niehs.nih.gov/kids/musicchild.htm
For music and lyrics to many favorite, traditional children's songs

FACT HOUND
Want more information about traditional songs? FACT HOUND offers a safe, fun way to find Web sites. All of the sites on Fact Hound have been researched by our staff. Simply follow these steps:

1. Visit *http://www.facthound.com*.
2. Enter a search word or 1404801499.
3. Click Fetch It.

Your trusty Fact Hound will fetch the best sites for you!